I'LL NEVER BE ASKED AGAIN

I'LL NEVER
BE ASKED AGAIN

TEXT AND DRAWINGS BY V H DRUMMOND
PREFACE BY LORD ALISTAIR GORDON
SCRIPT WRITTEN BY ALEXANDRA CULME-SEYMOUR

DEBRETT'S PEERAGE LTD

Text © V H Drummond 1979
Illustrations © V H Drummond 1979
All rights reserved

Published by Debrett's Peerage Ltd
23 Mossop Street, London sw3

Produced by Gulliver Press Ltd

TO MY HUSBAND

With thanks for his help and encouragement. And to our friends, without whose kind invitations to him to shoot in Scotland I would not have been able to write this book...But, having written it, I fear...
We'll never be asked again

Preface

MY COUSIN VIOLET (V. H. Drummond to you) has been writing grown-ups' children's books for forty years, so that the children she first wrote for are introducing *their* children to her books. The adventures of Mrs Easter or Little Laura do not date, because their gentle wit only pokes fun at the comedy of manners, because there is an air of the light fantastic, and, above all, because there is no pandering to social trendiness.

Revolutionaries and militants must fume and rage that their hatred for traditions and sacred cows is not as effective as the acute eye with which Violet observes the upper crust and their attendant nannies, cooks, gardeners, and game-keepers. Without malice or vilification she gives us sense and sensibility rather than pride and prejudice. Whereas Jane Austen could and did use her pen like a stiletto, Violet uses hers to tickle rather than to scratch. We are all familiar with the characters in this book — a few deft strokes and presto, there they are, encapsulated. How many Janes and Johnnies and Lady Alices and Colonel Glenlochys do we know! As for Bates the anti-hero, who has not been exasperated by one such as him?

Thirty-five years ago J. K. Stanford wrote a charming satire on grouse-shooting called The Twelfth. It was Violet's drawings that so ably enhanced the story and made it a classic of its kind.

Times have changed, but this has not been communicated to grouse, who still do their thing in the way they have always done. Grouse shooting is a peculiarly British activity because the red grouse is unique to the British Isles as Jonathan Ruffer so beautifully documented in his book The Big Shots. Its full development and the unwritten rules of the game came towards the end of the 19th century. Unfortunately this about coincided with the aristocracy's discovery that it had a social conscience and its attendant belief that to be comfortable is immoral.

The four-wheel drive cross-country vehicle has eliminated the discomfort of rocky and boggy walking, but the midges and flies are still there to torment in fine warm weather, and the rain to soak the thick obligatory tweeds and double their weight. And the shooting lodges from which the activities are planned have an austere functionalism undreamt of by the professors of the Bauhaus. They have bedrooms — even a few bathrooms, a large room in which to drink whisky and a rambling assortment of rooms at the back to house guns and to dry wet clothes and boots.

In recent times, influenced by marriage and transatlantic or Continental mores, some decadent grouse-shooters have introduced teams of cordon-bleu trained girls to cook, built more bathrooms, installed better heating, and even encouraged glamorous wives to attend the serious business of slaughtering grouse.

It is significant that the heroine of this tale is a Canadian. If she does eventually marry her Johnnie (which is more than likely) she will run his shooting lodge, if he has one, in a very different style to Lady Alice's ideas of comfort; and Bates will have to be tolerated as well, along with his friends.

Notwithstanding such gimmickery, I have a feeling (and so does Violet, I am sure) that it will still be plus ça change, plus c'est la même chose.

Alastair Gordon

When my parents and I arrived from Vancouver Island at the house we had rented in London, we found a dog resting on a chaise-longue in the drawing room.

The out going tenant told me that he was going to live in the country and that the dog, a spaniel called Bates, was a Londoner and the country life bored him to death.

To save him from this fate, I offered to keep him.

Bates and I were soon happily exploring London together.

Meanwhile my mother was busy with her Social Introductions.

"I want Jane to meet the RIGHT PEOPLE," she said.

That's how, at one of these deb. dances, I met Johnnie.

I liked Johnnie. We had a wonderful summer together.... dances, races, parties, theatres.....

Mother liked him... he was a super RIGHT PERSON, a Lord... who lived in a castle.

Bates hated him.

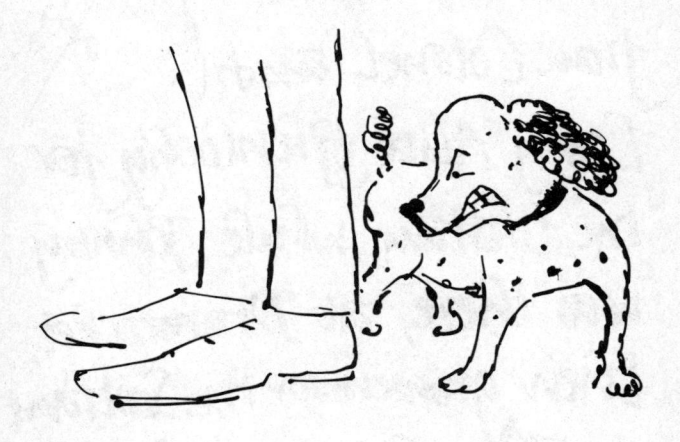

One evening Johnnie asked me to marry him.

Mother was overjoyed, but terribly anxious because I could not make up my mind. Then an invitation came from Colonel and Lady Alice Glenrocky for me to stay, while Johnny was there, at Drumrocket, their grousemoor in Scotland.
 This pleased Mother, a fortnight under the same roof should do the trick!

She hurried me off to buy some tweed skirts,

".... the RIGHT THING for the growemoor, my dear."

Johnnie's retriever was ill.

As I knew that Bates had once been to a gun-dog trainer, we decided to take him with us.

I only learnt later that the trainer had returned him saying that he was temperamentally unfit to be a gun-dog.

We travelled by
Night Train Motor Rail
to Scotland.
  After a restless night,
due to the jolting train,
and the shouting at
stations, I felt far from
my best as Johnnie and

I drove up to this bleak house, Drumrocket Lodge.

Lady Alice and Dinah, a labrador bitch, were in the hall.

One glance at Dinah and Bates became very over-excited, chased round and round after his tail... then lifted his leg against a table.

I was <u>horrified</u>
but Lady Alice took no
notice.

Though she did look
annoyed when he gobbled
up Dinah's breakfast.

The house party seemed
to know each other
frightfully well, though
some had only met the
night before.

They were eagerly discussing the various routes to Drumrocket.

Only the Ancient Uncle, who obviously disapproved of conversation at breakfast, was silent.

Lady Alice said to me:

"You'll be going out with the Guns this morning, I suppose?

We'll leave at nine thirty."

Out with the Guns! It sounded very WARLIKE.

I put on my warm pillar-box red coat with its hood trimmed with white fur.

"Good God!" exclaimed Lady Alice, "You're not coming out like that...
..... are you? You'll frighten every bird off the hill! Bimbo'll be furious!"

She, herself, was suitably clad in mud.

Colonel "Bimbo" Glencochy was not a bit furious.

But, surprisingly, Johnnie was!

I had to borrow a hideous mud-coloured garment from Lady Alice.

I didn't fancy myself in Mud.

The journey to the moor was a nightmare.

I wished Colonel Glenlochy would pay less attention to me and more to his driving.

"Marvellous vehicles these," he roared. "Go anywhere. Can't turn over!"

"It was just here," said Lady Alice coldly.

"that Jamie Strathrobert turned his car over last year... rolled down the hill..... finished upside-down in the burn".

I was thankful to get to that moor alive.

"What _are_ they doing," I asked, seeing the guns clustering round Colonel Glenlochy.

Anne, wife of the Glenlochy's son, Dougal, said:

"Bimbo's doing the draw.... so that they'll know which butt they're in in each drive.

"I don't think it works very well said another girl called Sally.

"Considering the number of times during the day you hear:

"What's my number? Which butt are _you_ in? Which butt am _I_ in?"

"The beaters start over there," explained Anne.

"And drive the grouse over those butts."

"How on earth do we get there?" I asked.

"Walk, of course," said Lady Alice.

Mother's RIGHT THING skirt seemed rather short for this exhausting activity.

The Ancient Uncle, lucky old man, rode by on the hill pony.

grumbling as he did so,
at the children who
clung to his stirrups.

Wire fences... should
one climb over...
under...
or through them?

25

Lady Alice, of course, vaulted over.

But she got into difficulties with some high barbed wire......

27

which Dinah was carried
over with loving care by
Colonel Glenlochy.

The Bottom Butt was reserved for the Ancient Uncle.

Exhausted, Bates and I staggered to the top.

"This floor's damn slippery," said Johnnie. "Please get

some dry heather for it."

Then he showed me how
to put cartridges into
his gun after he'd fired.

It was boring
waiting for
the birds...

then

suddenly... an ear-
-splitting BANG!

Johnnie had shot one..
It missed me by inches
but.....

.... crashed on to Bates's head.

"He's fainted," I cried, "Bates has fainted!"
"For God's sake keep quiet," hissed Johnnie, shoving the top half of his gun at me.

Very shaken, I completely forgot what I was supposed to do.

"Stick the cartridges in, blast you," yelled Johnnie.

As he closed his gun he hit me a terrific crack on the chin.

"Get out of the way, damn you," he shouted and blazed away.

When he thrust that horrible gun at me again... I accidentally stuffed my lipstick into it!

Furious, he flung it out muttering:

"I'll bloody well have to load for myself."

I opened my mouth to protest and a cartridge got ejected into it.

In agony I reeled backwards, upsetting the cartridge bag.

Cartridges cascaded everywhere.

Johnnie swore and tripped over Bates who let out a howl that must have been heard all down the line.

Mercifully, at that moment the whistle blew and the beaters approached.

"Did you mark my birds?" asked Johnnie.
"Mark them?"

"Yes. You should have watched where they fell."

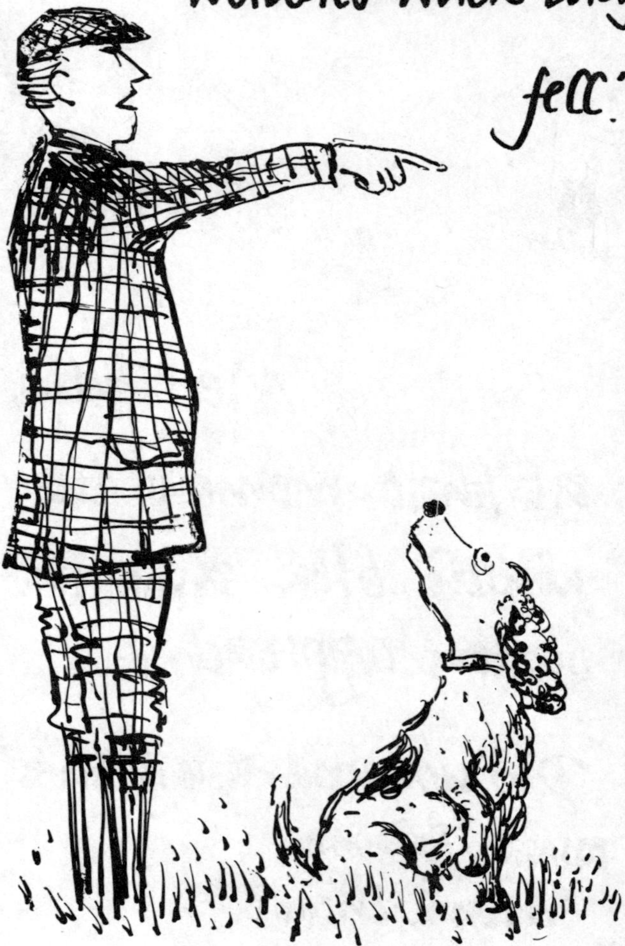

How did he think I had time to?

He pointed at Bates

"High lost" he said.

"High lost!

Go seek!"

Bates was bewildered by this extraordinary remark.

"This dog is useless... we'll have to find them ourselves."

A wounded bird fluttered in the heather. I screamed!

"Just conk it on the head," said Lady Alice disapprovingly.

"I couldn't, I just couldn't." With one deft movement she did it herself and...

...handed it to me to carry...
A n'auseating experience.

A very competitive spirit seemed to be around. Johnnie was about to pick up a bird when another gun said:

"I think that's mine."

"It is," I said, trying to be helpful, "I distinctly saw you shoot it."

The other gun walked off with it.

"How disloyal of you Jane," said Johnnie.

Bates, very pleased
with himself... picked
up a bird that Dinah,
who was considered the
best retriever in the
land, was looking for.

No one else seemed pleased

We discovered that Bates had been taking birds from Colonel Glenlochy's butt and putting them by Johnnie.

Now the Colonel really _was_ furions.

As we walked to the next drive, Sally told me about Mr. Wintz. "We all think it's safer to be with him than near him," she said.

Imagine how alarmed I was when I had to sit <u>outside</u> our butt because Lady Alice was inside - and I found Mr. Wintz was our neighbour.

"Mr. Wintz has shot me!" I screamed, as I felt myself lightly peppered.

"Never mention <u>who</u> shot you," said Lady Alice.

"There'd be room for me inside if Dinah came out," I pleaded.

"We can't risk Dinah being peppered," hissed Johnnie. "Stay where you are! There's another covey coming!"

An unpleasing change had come over him since we came to Drumrocket. He seemed to think of nothing else but how many grouse he was going to kill.

Crouching down amongst fronds of barbed wire, I don't know who was more frightened...... Bates or I.

Johnnie shot well in the next drive. I felt sorry for those poor little birds.

"Don't be silly," he said. "They enjoy it as much as we do."

Anyway the beaters seemed to enjoy themselves.

Even at lunch, Bates and I were in trouble. Me for feeding a bun to Dinah. Bates......... for lapping up Lady Alice's sloe gin.

54

"That's nice tweed,"
said one of the guns,
fingering my skirt.

   With dreadful snarls...
.... Bates saw him off.

   Anne laughed.
"He's known as the
Lecher," she said.

"He's got a reputation for making passes at girls in butts.

In Dongal's butt there was great mental

stress due to
overcrowding.

I offered to take
one of the children
to relieve congestion.

The little boy kept making remarks in loud whispers. Such as:

"Daddy would have got that one!"

At the end of the drive, for all to hear, he cried:

"Look! One Bird! Twenty cartridges!"

The Ancient Uncle eyed the child with displeasure. "In the good old days," he muttered, "women and children were not tolerated on this moor."

That afternoon we were plagued by midges. "Light a small fire," said Johnnie, "Smoke'll keep 'em off."

I managed to light a small fire with dry heather, an old cigarette packet and sweet papers

But I blew too hard on it and set the whole butt alight.

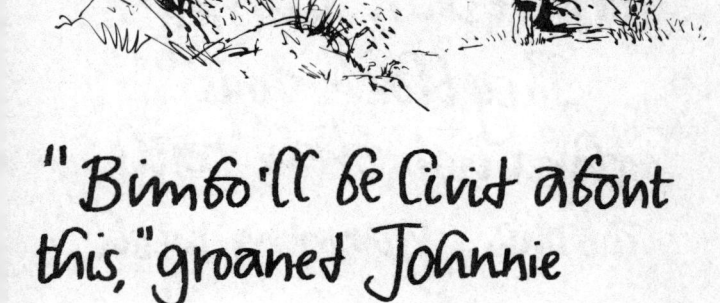

"Bimbo'll be livid about this," groaned Johnnie

I sat at the back of the landrover for the return journey. Big black dogs thrashed their tails about.... yawning, with wide open mouths... and terrible breath.

Colonel Glenlochy drove with his usual recklessness and once the Landrover lurched so much from side to side that we were all thrown on top of each other.

I landed in the arms of the Lecher, who didn't release me till Bates, with dreadful snarls intervened.

After my bath, I hung my bra and pants in the Drying Room.

The Ancient Uncle
Came tottering in.

"Women!
women!"

he growled.
"I never thought I'd live to see Drumrocket invaded by <u>women</u>."

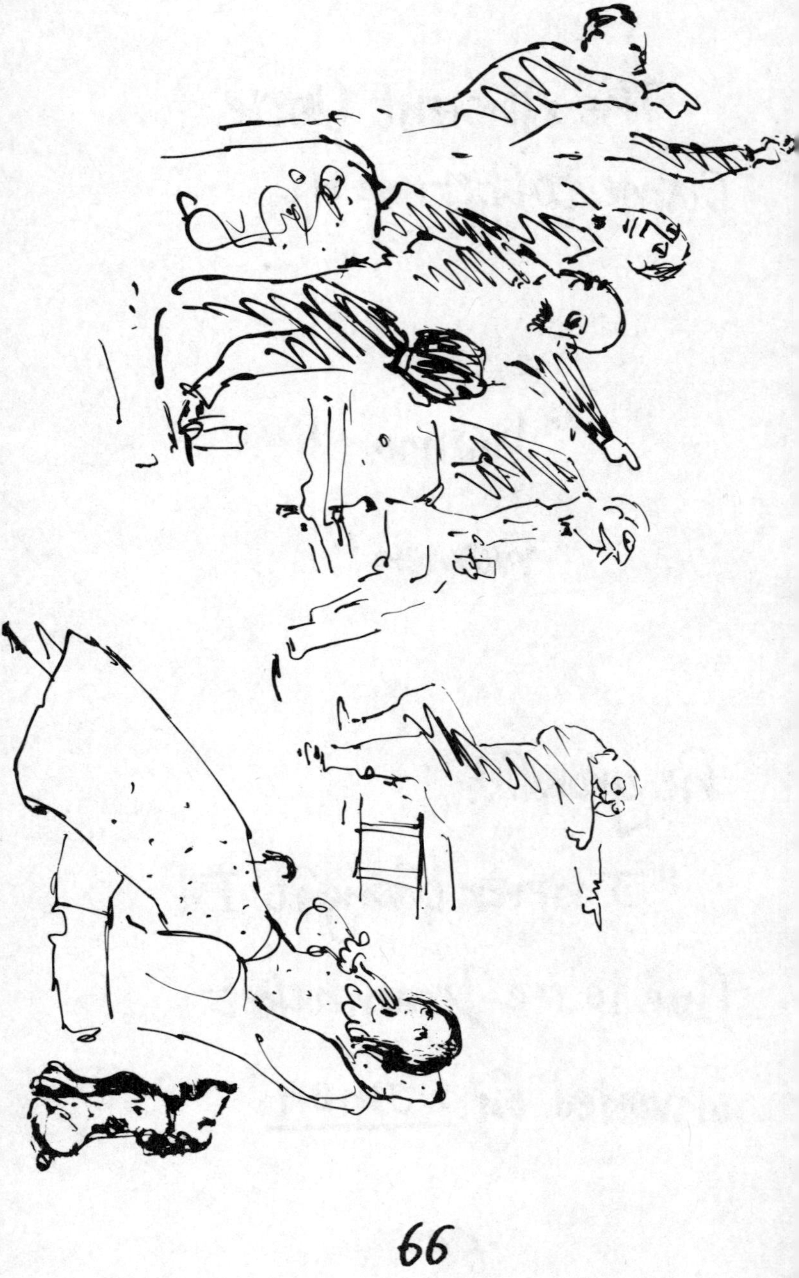

That evening, the guns relived every moment of the day.

At dinner, Bates, noticing Colonel Glenlochy stroking my knee, flew out from under the table and started his dreadful snarling at him.

"I can't imagine why that dog should attack poor old Bimbo like that," said Lady Alice.

"Nor can I," said the Lecher, untruthfully.

Next morning it was pelting with rain. Lady Alice arranged for women and children to join the guns at lunch time.

At 12:30 it was still raining. "We can't possibly go out like this" I thought, joyfully.

But Lady Alice appeared wearing a monstrous rain hat.

"We'll have to go" murmured Sally, "there'll be no lunch here."

Bates, he stayed by the fire.

Cold and hungry
we searched the moor...

Our heroes didn't seem to have missed us much.

What a sight I looked!

Luckily Johnnie was too preoccupied to notice.

What a way to spend a holiday!

Next day was lovely...
a walking-up day.
But Johnnie spoilt it
by saying:
"Keep in line."
"Don't moon about."

And Bates was in a bad temper because he had to be on a lead.

We leapt over a little stream and I fell in.

All Johnnie did was to say:

"For God's sake... KEEP UP."

But I'd dropped Bates's lead and he bounded in front of the line.

Happy to be free..... he expressed himself by rolling in some black mud then leaping joyously over a fence, which, unfortunately, Colonel Glenlochy was just approaching.

The two collided........
and, with fearful oaths
the Colonel fell to the ground.

Bates shook himself vigorously.

Then, barking gaily,
went off to chase a
 passing hare,

putting
up coveys of grouse in
all directions.

The chase ended when the hare turned and faced him.

"That damned dog!" groaned Johnnie, "I'll never be asked again."

"That dog must GO!"
roared Bimbo Glenlochy,
red with rage, and
ordered Bates off the moor!

A traumatic moment for me.

If Bates must go.....

I must go.

I looked at Johnnie.

"Take your blasted dog away,"

he muttered.

And moved on with the line.

A grouse stood up in the heather crying:

"Go back!
Go back!"

Lady Alice said:
"There's many a woman trudging the moor this day who wouldn't be doing so had they had pre-marital experience of grouse shooters."

She sighed, then strode forward to join Bimbo.

Back at the lodge I found Sally, packing to go home.

"Men are often preoccupied, off-hand and aggressive

on the moor" she said,
" You get used to it."
    Get used to it?
Not ME.
  I composed a letter to
Lady Alice:
.... Urgent message etc. etc. ...
must return home immediately"
  Then off to London with
  Sally.
    Poor Mother!
No wedding! No castles!
No coronets!
    But now, whenever I
think of Lady Alice

trudging through thick, wet, heather, suitably clad in mud, I am truly grateful to......

... my dear, darling Bates.